The Adventures of Charlie the Bulldog at Camp

Cover design by el Emma afia.

This book was typeset in Emma afia.

First edition, 2023.

Published by Emma Afia.

Chapter 1: Getting Ready for Camp

- Charlie is excited to go on his first camping trip with his human family
- His family packs the car with all the essentials for camping
- Charlie wonders what adventures await him in the great outdoors

Chapter 2: Arrival at the Campsite

- Charlie and his family arrive at the campsite and set up their tent
- Charlie explores the campsite and meets some new animal friends
- He learns about the importance of staying safe in the wilderness

Chapter 3: A Hike in the Woods

- Charlie and his family go on a hike in the woods
- Charlie gets separated from his family and has to find his way back to the campsite
- He uses his sense of smell and his intuition to navigate the forest and reunite with his family

Chapter 4: The Campfire Story

- Charlie and his family sit around the campfire and tell spooky stories
- Charlie gets scared and learns that it's okay to be afraid sometimes
- His family reassures him and teaches him how to be brave

Chapter 5: Saying Goodbye to Camp

- Charlie and his family pack up and say goodbye to the campsite
- Charlie is sad to leave his new animal friends behind but is excited to go home
- He reflects on all the fun and valuable experiences he had at camp and looks forward to his next adventure.

Chapter 1: Getting Ready for Camp

Charlie could hardly contain his excitement as he watched his human family pack up the car for their first camping trip. He'd heard all about the great outdoors and couldn't wait to explore it for himself.

His family loaded up the car with a tent, sleeping bags, coolers, and all sorts of camping gear. Charlie watched as they packed his own bag with his food, water, and a cozy blanket to sleep on.

"Are you ready for an adventure, Charlie?" his human dad asked, giving him a pat on the head. Charlie barked and wagged his tail, eager to get going. He hopped into the car and settled into the back seat, watching as the scenery outside the window changed from city streets to forests and mountains.

As they drove, Charlie wondered what exciting things he would discover at the campsite. He imagined hiking through the woods, chasing squirrels, and maybe even swimming in a cool lake.

Finally, after what seemed like hours of driving, they arrived at the campsite. Charlie's tail wagged furiously as he leaped out of the car and ran around, taking in all the sights and smells.

His family set up the tent while Charlie explored the campsite. He met a friendly chipmunk who showed him where the best acorns were, and a wise old owl who warned him about the dangers of wandering too far from camp.

As the sun began to set, Charlie curled up in his blanket, exhausted but content. He knew that the adventures of the next few days would be ones he would never forget.

Chapter 2: Arrival at the Campsite

The next morning, Charlie woke up to the sound of birds chirping and a cool breeze blowing through the tent. He was eager to start exploring the campsite.

His human family made breakfast over the campfire, and Charlie eagerly licked his lips as he smelled the bacon sizzling in the pan. After breakfast, they went for a walk around the campsite.

Charlie was amazed by all the sights and sounds. He saw tall trees that stretched up to the sky and flowers of every color blooming in the meadows. He also met some new animal friends, including a friendly raccoon and a family of rabbits.

As they walked, Charlie's human mom pointed out some of the hazards that could be dangerous for a curious dog like Charlie. She showed him how to avoid poison ivy, stay away from prickly cactus plants, and how to safely cross streams.

After their walk, Charlie was tired but happy. He curled up under a tree for a nap while his family set up the tent for the night.

As the sun began to set, Charlie sat with his family around the campfire. They roasted marshmallows and told stories about their day. Charlie was amazed by all the adventures he had already had, and he knew that there were many more to come.

Chapter 3: A Hike in the Woods

The next day, Charlie's human family decided to go on a hike in the woods. Charlie was thrilled to explore the wilderness and see what other animals he could meet.

They packed a backpack with water, snacks, and a map, and headed out on the trail. Charlie led the way, his nose sniffing the air as he took in all the new scents.

As they walked, Charlie's family pointed out different plants and animals along the way. They saw a deer grazing in a clearing and a family of squirrels playing in the trees. Charlie loved every minute of the hike, but he soon realized he had wandered off the trail and couldn't see his family anywhere. He barked and whined, but no one answered.

Charlie was scared and didn't know what to do. He sat down and tried to think of a way to find his family. He remembered that his human dad had said that he should try to stay in one place if he ever got lost. Charlie decided to wait right where he was until his family found him. He curled up under a tree and waited, listening for any sounds of his family coming to find him.

After what seemed like hours, Charlie heard a familiar voice calling his name. He barked back, and soon his family appeared, looking worried and relieved to find him safe. Charlie was overjoyed to be reunited with his family, and they continued their hike back to the campsite. Charlie learned a valuable lesson that day about staying safe in the wilderness and the importance of staying close to his family.

Chapter 4: The Campfire Story

That night, after dinner, Charlie's human family gathered around the campfire. They roasted marshmallows and shared stories about their day. Charlie was content to listen to the stories, but he wanted to share one of his own. He barked and whined until his family realized he had a story to tell. They gathered around him, eager to hear what he had to say.

Charlie started to tell the story of how he met his best friend, a stray cat who lived in his neighborhood. He told them about how they would play together and explore the alleys and backyards of the neighborhood.

Charlie's family was amazed by his story, and they all laughed and smiled as he told it. When he finished, they all clapped and gave him a pat on the head.

As the night wore on, Charlie's family told more stories, each one more exciting than the last. They shared their dreams and hopes for the future, and Charlie felt grateful to be a part of such a wonderful family.

Finally, it was time to go to bed. Charlie snuggled up in his blanket and drifted off to sleep, dreaming of all the adventures still waiting for him at camp.

Chapter 5: Saying Goodbye to Camp

The last day of camp arrived, and Charlie was sad to leave. He had had so many adventures and made so many new friends, he didn't want it to end.

Charlie's family started to pack up their things and take down the tent. Charlie watched them, feeling a sense of sadness wash over him.

But as they were packing up, Charlie's new animal friends started to appear, each one saying goodbye and promising to see him again. The raccoon brought him a pinecone, and the rabbits brought him some fresh grass to chew on.

Charlie's family saw how much these animals meant to him and decided to stay a little longer so that he could say goodbye to all of them properly.

Finally, it was time to go. Charlie said goodbye to his new friends, knowing he would miss them dearly. As they drove away from the campsite, Charlie looked out the window, feeling a sense of nostalgia for the adventures they had all shared. But as they drove, Charlie's family started to plan their next adventure. They talked excitedly about all the places they could go and all the things they could see. Charlie felt his tail wagging with excitement, knowing that the adventures were just beginning.

As they pulled into their driveway, Charlie couldn't wait to tell his other animal friends about all the adventures he had had. He knew that the memories of camp would stay with him forever, and he felt grateful for the experiences and the love of his family.

The End

This is a work of fiction. Names, characters, businesses, organizations, places, events, and incidents either are the product of the author's imagination or are used fictitiously. Any resemblance to actual persons, living or dead, events, or locales is entirely coincidental.

The following trademarked terms are mentioned in this book: Mohamed El Afia. The use of these trademarks does not indicate an endorsement of this work by the trademark owners. The trademarks are used in a purely descriptive sense and all trademark rights remain with the trademark owner.

Cover design by el Emma afia.

This book was typeset in Emma afia.

First edition, 2023.

Published by Emma Afia.

Made in United States
Troutdale, OR
12/18/2023

16059794R00018